MIDNIGHT FEASTS

MIDNIGHT FEASTS
An Anthology of Late-Night Munchies

Selected and Introduced by Charmain Ponnuthurai
Illustrated by Laurie Bellanca

midnight, n.
1. A. The middle of the night; spec. (now the usual sense) 12 o'clock at night.
   B. An instance or occurrence of midnight.
2. Intense darkness or gloom; a period of intense darkness.
3. fig. The crucial hour, the moment when something
   reaches a crisis or comes to an end.

feast, n.
An unusually abundant and delicious meal; something delicious to feed upon;
fig. an exquisite gratification, a rich treat.

For Barnaby Tuke

CONTENTS

INTRODUCTION

First midnight feasts are reminiscent of Enid Blyton's *The Ship of Adventure*. It was getting quite dark now. The sun had gone a long time ago, and the children could hardly see one another as they sat together in the courtyard, munching hungrily. "I've never known bread and cheese to taste so lovely", said Diana.
"It's goat-milk cheese, isn't it, Bill?
I say, look at Micky stuffing himself."

Midnight feasts are a delicious opportunity to indulge the senses away from the rules of the table and the constraints of recipes and courses. After dark, the clock takes a backseat, and life takes on the quality of Toy Town. Nothing presses from the day's deadlines and interruptions, and the belief grows that maybe Peter Pan and Neverland are not just the stuff of fairy tales. Eating with fingers, crossed-legged on the floor, or straight from the fridge, one flavour following bizarrely on another, is suddenly allowed. This book is a celebration of late-night eating, alone, with friends or lovers, on leftovers and favourite treats, or spontaneously throwing a few ingredients together in a moment of delectable therapy. You could be under the cover of starry skies or wrapped in the comfort of your duvet, the rules are up to you.

Whether memories or fantasies, these moments are a delight to recreate, and now that I have children, even more so. Early experiences of secretly raiding the food supplies, exploring the freedom to eat what we like the most without the table etiquette forced on us by elders and betters, are how we first strike up a sense of our individual palette. This childlike sense of identity through taste and smell is for me, considering the pressures and demands of our daily lives, one essential way to unwind.

The midnight feast is a time in which to get old-fashioned about food, to ignore the rules that tell us what goes with what, and forget about health warnings and calorie counts. Late at night provides an unrivalled time to take to the doorstop of your home or gaze from the window at the world at rest, free-forming thoughts and ideas with a platter of delicious morsels to munch on. In the quiet of night, with nothing but our senses to guide us, we can enjoy the thought that it is the simple things that count.

My love of late-night eating began with a feast of small juicy Cox's apples, a slice of Colston Basset stilton, and a handful of walnuts, all wrapped in waxed paper and eagerly eaten in the early hours of the morning after a long train journey. It was the start of a love affair, and soon became a ritual at midnight or in the small hours, the two of us snacking on leftover roasted peppers with preserved lemons and jars of anchovies, tucking into cheeses, cold meats, olives, grapes, nuts and chocolate. These might be washed down with a glass of wine, a creamy scoop of homemade vanilla ice cream, or else soothing teas like chamomile, rose petal or verbena, or simply oodles of full fat cold milk.

Intrigued to see what nocturnal adventures others had with food, I began asking about their first food forays at midnight. Sophie Conran remembered her favourite munchies at midnight as a tasty fry-up followed by hot chocolate, ladled with cream and fresh chocolate gratings with a best pal. I then discovered a whole a mix of stories, involving sardines under bed covers, fish bakes wrapped up in red ribbons, sweet treats like chocolate lollies with red velvet insides, and simple comforts like spaghetti with chilli. As you leaf your way through this notebook of midnight feasts, you will find a mixture of flavours and ideas. Some involve little more than opening your fridge door, while others offer a clever marriage of ingredients to create something sensuous and surprising. Try the tasty tapas of Moro's 'Chorizo with Sherry' or Ottolenghi's blissful 'Peaches and Burrata Cheese'. Or cook up a more elaborate feast, sometimes the perfect antidote to the day's troubles. Use this book when you want to fulfil urgent cravings and follow these suggestions to discover the horizons of your own tastes.

Just as anyone can feast at midnight, whether or not they can cook, so these pages contain dishes not only from food writers and chefs but also from people engaged in a variety of other professions, including fashion, gardening, sport, design and music. They include contributions from actress Gillian Anderson, accessories designer Anya Hindmarch, chef Fergus Henderson of St Johns and writer Meg Rosoff, all of whom share tasty dishes and memories of past midnight feasts, in aid of Springboard, the children's dyslexia charity.

Charmain Ponnuthurai

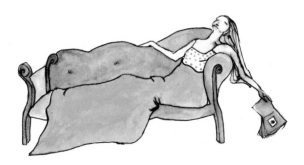

1

Food for Eating in Bed

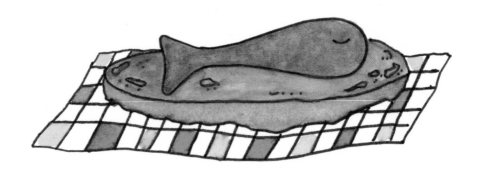

FERGUS HENDERSON'S SARDINES
ON TOAST IN BED

This sensory midnight feast was taught to me by a wise old chef — sardines on toast eaten in bed in the dark.

My earliest memory of late-night eating was of working my way through a sack of pistachio nuts late into the night as the parents jollied away. Now I would enjoy sitting on a rock in the Hebrides with Margot, my wife, eating Fruit and Nut, drinking malt whisky and being blown about by the wind.

Also it is strange how appealing mini bars of Toblerone can become between the hours of 12 and 3am.

INGREDIENTS
• a few slices of brown bread • butter as desired • tin of sardines • half a lemon

METHOD
Toast your brown bread, butter liberally and then squidge the tinned sardines onto your bread with a fork. Add a healthy squeeze of lemon, turn the light off and get into bed and eat.
Serves 1

Yotam Ottolenghi's Burrata with Flat White Peach

The point of this dish is the meeting of two incredible ingredients, both luscious and sensual, combined with no distractions from anything else. It's pure, simple and amazingly delicious. At some point in July you can come across this odd yet beautifully formed flat white peach from France. It is sweet, not very acidic and has just the right degree of juiciness to make it an ideal counterpart to cheese. It looks like a real fruit should — slightly misshapen, irregular and asymmetrical. The cheese I have in mind is burrata from Puglia. It is also beautifully ugly — shaped like a little bumpy sack, tied with a green knot — and is creamier than mozzarella. In fact, it is so creamy and so unctuously rich you might be satisfied with just a little bit of it. Breaking the outer, firmish casing, you encounter a buttery centre made of fresh cream and unspun mozzarella curds.

INGREDIENTS
• 2 flat white peaches (at room temperature) • as much as you want of a 300g burrata ball • best extra virgin olive oil • Maldon sea salt and freshly ground black pepper (optional)

METHOD
No rules should actually apply here. You cut the peaches into wedges or any other shape, break a piece of burrata, spoon on top and drizzle with a little oil. This is heavenly, with or without extra seasoning.
Serves 1 or 2

Don Foster's Crème Fraîche & Plain Yoghurt with Brown Sugar

Aged 11, at scout camp, I remember sitting around a bonfire eating dough wrapped around sticks and cooked in the fire while singing amazingly silly songs. Nowadays I'd still favour an open fire with friends and family gathered round late on a summer night with great food, wine and Bob Dylan in the background. If I keep practising I may soon serenade my guests on my newly acquired ukulele. Sadly it's more often the chimes of Big Ben on Radio 4 waiting for the midnight news.

INGREDIENTS
• plain yoghurt (amount optional but must equal quantity of cream used)
double cream or crème fraîche • soft brown sugar

METHOD
Mix equal quantities of plain yoghurt and double cream (or crème fraîche for the squeamish). Sprinkle soft brown sugar on top. Leave in fridge for as long as you can wait before eating.
Serves 1

Gillian Anderson's Peanut Butter & a Banana

Here's a midnight snack that requires a little bit of forethought.

INGREDIENTS
• 1 banana • 2 tablespoons peanut butter

METHOD
Take the banana and slice it end to end down the middle. Take some peanut butter, smooth or crunchy, your choice, and lather it down one side of the banana as thick as your taste desires. Place the other half of the banana on top like a sandwich.

Then slice two, three or four times, depending on the size of your banana, creating little individual peanut butter banana sandwiches. Wrap each section individually in tin foil and place the whole lot of them in a plastic container in the freezer. Then, in the middle of the night, open the freezer, grab a ball of tinfoil, unwrap it, and find a surprisingly delicious snack just waiting for your enjoyment. The image that most reminds me of this snack is the yellow man that pops up when you send an AOL email message.

Serves 1

2

Food for Eating
by the Fridge Light

Sophie Conran's Late-Night Salad

When I was a child, we had amazing eggs from our own chickens, as well as milk that I would collect in a pail from a local farm. Midnight feasts generally involved fried eggs and bacon on toast and hot chocolate. My friend Gemma would come and stay the night and we would sneak downstairs together. I lived in a large house and it was a long way from the bedroom to the kitchen. We would make hot chocolate using Cadbury's cocoa powder with heated milk, whipped cream and fresh chocolate grated on top — our idea of heaven. Hot chocolate and a fry-up make an amazing midnight feast, but nowadays I tend to have a midnight feast due to working late and forgetting to eat. My last midnight feast was a rather tasty salad, thrown together from the bits and bobs in the fridge.

INGREDIENTS
• large handful of herby salad • drizzle of home-made mayonnaise • a smoked mackerel fillet, cut into chunks • various veg (e.g. parsnip, sweet potato and acorn squash, that has been roasted in olive oil and a teaspoon of garam masala) • sprinkling of fresh chopped tarragon and a grind of black pepper

METHOD
Mix ingredients together in a bowl. Wash this all down with a cup of chamomile tea.
Serves 1

Anya Hindmarch's Platter
of Cold Meat
& Potted Artichokes

My midnight feast would be taken straight from the fridge and shared with my husband James, my five children and any friends that happened to be at home. As I don't cook, this would have to be a platter of my favourite cold meats, ideally accompanied with some potted artichokes.

INGREDIENTS
• platter of cold charcuterie meats from local deli • jar of potted artichokes

METHOD
Lay meats on plate and add as many artichokes as you wish.
Serves 1 or more

SAM HART'S BROWN SHRIMPS ON TOAST

My favourite memory of midnight feasts is of the Taco stands in Mexico City with tacky mariachi music on a tinny radio with my wife, Robin. I am a very hungry person so the idea of a midnight feast has always appealed to me.

INGREDIENTS
• 4 small pots of brown shrimps • 4 slices quality sour dough bread (ideally Poilâne) • 125g quality butter • 2 teaspoons cayenne pepper • 1 pinch nutmeg • 1 pinch mace • 1 lemon • 1 bunch fresh chives • 75ml quality extra virgin olive oil • pepper to taste

METHOD
Firstly slice the sour dough bread 1cm thick and chargrill. Butter the toast and place a handful of shrimps on each slice, sprinkle with the cayenne, mace and nutmeg.
Sprinkle with fresh lemon juice and add a few turns of black pepper. Serve with a simple baby gem salad. Dress with a little olive oil, lemon juice and chopped chives.
Serves 2

Eric Treuille's Poilâne Bread & Cabecous Goat's Cheese Delights

I remember being 6 years old and finishing a roast chicken whilst sitting in the dark with the dog, drinking milk and juice and then being woken up the next morning on the kitchen floor. Nowadays, I listen to loud, very loud Wagner, which sounds dramatic and provides a suitably sensory companion for cold meat and mayonnaise. Or, I sit on the table with the fridge door open for light and drink a bottle of good Savarine. The moment Radio 4 switches to the World Service is a brilliant reminder of the arrival of midnight.

I do think leftover dishes, cold meat, roasted vegetables and gratin dishes are underrated. They provide the most wonderful feast from the fridge at night, as they give you very different flavours, served with a full panel of condiments, sauces and pickles. The best way is to serve and eat with your fingers, but, most importantly, to eat lots.

INGREDIENTS
• 2 slices Poilâne bread, toasted • 1 clove of garlic, peeled • 1 tablespoon of olive oil • 2 cabecous (rounded individual goat cheese — make sure they are creamy) • 1 tablespoon of runny honey • good cracked black pepper

METHOD
Rub the peeled garlic on the toasted bread and drizzle a tablespoon of olive oil on the toast. Add the cheese and a tablespoon of honey. Grill on medium heat for two minutes then spread the warmed cheese evenly over the bread and add black pepper. Enjoy.
Serves 1

PRUE LEITH'S MUSCOVADO HEAVEN

At boarding schools all over Africa the midnight feast was tinned sardines with sweetened condensed milk. Could there be anything more disgusting? Yet we ate it, with relish. But here's a recipe that would be easy to assemble on a dormitory floor.

INGREDIENTS
• 4 tablespoons of plain yoghurt • 2 tablespoons of condensed milk or custard
• 1 tablespoon of dark Muscovado sugar

METHOD
Tip two inches of plain yoghurt into each person's toothmug. Then add an inch of double cream or custard and mix. Sprinkle with a tablespoon of dark Muscovado sugar. Put the mugs aside while you eat everything else. By the time you get to the pud, the sugar will be half treacly sauce and half delicious crunch.
PS. Only dark Muscovado gives the right flavour!
Serves 1

Meg Rosoff's Midnight Hummus

I find the part of the day when emails stop arriving, the phone doesn't ring and the rest of the family is asleep, the most productive time for writing. I work until after 1am at least two or three times a week, despite being the sort of person who needs lots of sleep and would rather be in bed by 9. And what with dinner receding into the dim and distant past, and no emails to check for a break, I've been known to pad down to the kitchen (followed by my loyal lurchers) and prepare something to munch on. Don't get the wrong idea — if there are biscuits, I'll go for the easy option. But too often there are no biscuits, and that's when hummus and pitta bread spring to the fore.

It takes approximately 5 minutes to make and yields enough for days.

INGREDIENTS
• 2 cans of chickpeas, with the liquid from about half a can • 2 huge tablespoons of tahini • 1 tablespoon of sesame seeds (if you have them) • 2-10 garlic cloves (to taste, and depending on bed partner!) • 1 tablespoon olive oil • juice of one small lemon • salt to taste

METHOD
Whiz everything in a blender until smoothish, but not too smooth. Toast a whole wheat pitta bread, put a couple of big dollops of hummus on a plate with the pitta bread, make a nice cup of tea, then go back to work!
Serves 1

DUNCAN CAMPBELL'S AVOCADO & WORCESTER SAUCE

My own favourite for a midnight feast is avocado with Lea and Perrins Worcester Sauce accompanied by some soothing John Prine music.

INGREDIENTS
• 1 large avocado, ripe • Worcester sauce • lemon juice, a squeeze

METHOD
Cut the avocado in half, sprinkle liberally with Worcester sauce and squeeze plenty of lemon juice onto it.
Serves 1

Greek yoghurt
Digestive Biscuits
Lemon Juice
Nuts & Almonds

Cheese Cake's Girl Night

RACHEL JOHNSON'S INSTANT CHEESECAKE

I'm a bowl-of-cereal girl when it comes to midnight feasts, or I just open the freezer and grab a tub of Ben and Jerry's and stand there mindlessly spooning it into my mouth until I'm sated… If I'm hungry I'll eat anything. Cold spaghetti. Oatibix straight from the packet. Oatcakes with butter and jam are great too — especially at midnight with a cup of sleepytime herbal tea.

INGREDIENTS
• 1-2 tablespoons of Greek yoghurt • 1 tablespoon lemon juice • 2 digestive biscuits • 1 tablespoon soft dark brown sugar • sprinkling of toasted walnuts and almonds

METHOD
Plop some Greek yoghurt in the bottom of a bowl — add a good squirt of lemon juice, mix, then crush a digestive biscuit or two and sprinkle over the yoghurt. Add one heaped spoon of soft dark brown sugar and, if you feel like it, some toasted walnuts or toasted flaked almonds... YUM
Serves 1

3

Friends to Feast With

Gwyneth Paltrow's Capon, Grandma Style & Chinese Duck

Spain... a Culinary Road Trip (Ecco, 2008)

Capon, Grandma Style

INGREDIENTS
• ¾ cup olive oil • 1 bunch Italian parsley, leaves removed and chopped
• 2 garlic cloves, thinly sliced • 1 tablespoon kosher salt • 10-pound capon
cut into 14 pieces • 1 cup cognac or other brandy • 3 cups dry red wine
• 2 Spanish onions, cut into 8 wedges each

METHOD
Combine ½ cup of the olive oil, the parsley, garlic and salt in a blender and
zap until smooth. Put the capon in a baking dish or shallow bowl and pour the
parsley mixture over it, turning to coat. Cover and marinate at room temperature
for 2 hours, or for as long as overnight in the refrigerator.
Heat a large heavy pot over medium-high heat, then add the remaining ¼ cup
of the olive oil and heat until hot. Working in batches, add the capon, skin side
down, and cook until deep golden brown on the first side, about 7 minutes.
Turn and cook until deep brown on the second side, about 7 more minutes.
Return all the capon to the pot, add the cognac, and boil until reduced by half.
Add the wine and boil until reduced by one-third. Add the onions and bring to
a simmer, then lower the heat to a gentle simmer, cover, and cook for 2 hours,
until the meat is almost falling off the bone.
Serves 8 to 10

Chinese Duck

INGREDIENTS
• 10-pound organic duck cut into 14 pieces (see Capon, Grandma Style above)
• 3-4 garlic cloves • cloves, ground • black pepper • one cup Madeira • one cup
sake • fresh ginger, grated • a sprinkle of sugar • mirin • 2 star anise • olive oil
• soy sauce • cilantro, chopped • scallions, sliced

METHOD
Get a very good organic duck. Cut it into 14 pieces. Prick the skin all over with
a sharp paring knife. Rub with some softened butter that's been mixed with 3
or 4 minced garlic cloves. Sprinkle with ground cloves and black pepper. Brown
the duck well in olive oil in a large heavy pot. Pour off all but a few tablespoons
of the fat and add a cup each of Madeira and sake, some mirin, a sprinkle of
sugar, lots of grated fresh ginger, a few crushed garlic cloves, and 2 star anise.
Bring to a boil, then lower the heat to a gentle simmer, cover, and cook for 3
hours, or until the duck is very tender. During the last 10 minutes, add soy sauce
to taste. Serve garnished with tons of chopped cilantro and sliced scallions.
Serves 8 to 10

Sally Clarke's Shrimp
& Courgette Flower Risotto

Staying up late at night began as a teenager during my first holiday with school friends in Cornwall. After a long camper van journey we ate the most divinely delicious fish and chips out of newspaper at midnight. I can still taste them!

If I were to stay up late now it would be with Richard Strauss, probably at home in the country by a wood-burning fire with my husband and 9-year-old son. These days though, I am too tired for the idea of a midnight feast — even on New Year's Eve.

A risotto, to me, is not only comforting to make and stir but also to eat. Although the recipe looks a little daunting, it is relatively simple to make and as long as you have the ingredients prepared and ready, it can be made in 15-20 minutes. If shrimp are not available use small chunks of fresh or smoked fish or just keep it vegetarian using vegetable stock and mushrooms, asparagus, peas or fava beans. There are endless choices.

INGREDIENTS
• 1 tablespoon good olive oil • 70g butter, at room temperature • 1 medium onion, finely diced • 175g Arborio or Carnaroli rice • 125ml dry white wine • 150ml vegetable or fish stock • 125g courgette, diced • salt and pepper • 300g shrimp, cooked in the shell, or 300g shrimp, cooked and peeled • 3 courgette flowers, chopped (or any garden herb flower would be fine such as: nasturtium; chive, snipped at top; rocket leaf — or just add extra courgette, if needed, or sliced field mushrooms cooked with the onion if no flowers available) • 1 teaspoon tarragon

METHOD
In a heavy-based pan, warm the olive oil with 35g butter until melted. Over a gentle heat, stir in the onion and cook until transparent. Add the rice and continue to cook until the grains of rice are thoroughly coated in the oil. Turn up the heat a little and stir in the wine. When the wine has almost completely evaporated, gradually start stirring in the stock, a ladleful at a time, stirring continuously and then add the courgettes, courgette flowers, tarragon and shrimp.
Serves 2

Concerto in
Risotto Major
for Shrimp &
Courgette flower

ULYSSE & CIRCÉ

in the Sky

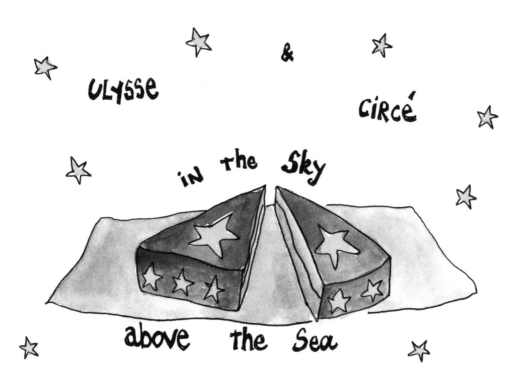

above the Sea

Rose Gray's Chocolate & Ginger Cake

My perfect midnight feast was taken lying on the roof of Casa Nettuna in San Felice Circeo, south of Rome. We watched the stars, overlooking the sea with the Island of Ponza in the distance, eating chocolate cake!

INGREDIENTS
• 200g fresh root ginger • 500g unsalted butter, plus extra for greasing
• 500g bitter-sweet Callebaut chocolate, with a minimum of 70% cocoa solids
• 70g fine polenta flour • 2 tablespoons cocoa powder • 10 medium organic free range eggs • 400g caster sugar • a pinch of baking powder

METHOD
Preheat the oven to 150°C. Butter and line a 30cm cake tin with parchment paper. Melt the chocolate and butter together in a bowl over a pan of simmering water. Do not let the bowl touch the water. Peel and finely chop the ginger and add the chocolate mixture, once it has melted, along with the flour and cocoa powder. Allow to cool a little.

In a mixer combine the eggs and sugar and whisk until they have trebled in volume. Slowly fold the whisked eggs, sugar and baking powder into the chocolate mixture. Pour into the prepared tin and bake in the preheated oven for 45 minutes. When the cake is cooked, place a plate on the top for 5 minutes. This will give the cake a good dense texture.

Serves 12

Seabass' Song

Guo Yue's Steamed Sea Bass
with Ginger

When I returned to the Beijing alleys after the death of Mao in 1977, having travelled all over China as an army musician, Deng Xiaoping began to give a little more freedom to the Chinese: for me, this meant the pleasure of spending evenings dancing with girls, for the first time. Under Mao, you were not allowed to love. Afterwards, around midnight, I would go with friends to a tiny restaurant which made hun-tun tang (little dumpling soup) in front of you, in a huge steaming wok. We would sit and watch this beautiful traditional art form in action, seated on simple wooden benches at simple wooden tables. We talked about our dreams, our longing for freedom, and the places we wanted to travel to, beyond the closed doors of China. Then we would walk home through the alleys, singing and smoking, before bidding each other goodnight. In those days, the skies of Beijing were full of stars.

My memories of midnight are of my four sisters lined up like matches — four of them across one bed, with their feet balanced on chairs — and my mother, brother and me in the other room, next to the cooking stove! A lot of whispering, snoring and sometimes shouting, mostly at the crickets I kept under my bed — they loved to sing at night! My mother would sit up in bed, eating her favourite dish of hong shao rou (red stewed pork with noodles) with chopsticks, and telling us stories of her childhood in Harbin, on the border with Russia.

A midnight feast should be delicious, sensual and seductive — easy to prepare, with a freshness and lightness and that will not interrupt your dreams. There is something splendid about this dish but at the same time it is about simplicity — keeping the cool, delicate essence of the fish and enhancing it with the intense heat of ginger, an ingredient known in ancient China as a powerful aphrodisiac! Chinese food often creates a balance between opposites: a harmony that has its parallels with music. Serve with steamed Basmati rice.

INGREDIENTS
• a good-sized sea bass, cleaned and scaled • 3-4 spring onions — just the white part — cut into very fine strips • fresh root ginger • light soy sauce • white caster sugar • chinese cooking rice wine • sunflower oil • 2 fresh red chillis, the long slender ones (optional)

METHOD
Begin by diagonally scoring the fish on both sides. Put a thin slice of ginger into each slash. Then steam in a bamboo steamer for 10-15 minutes, until the flesh becomes beautifully white. Remove and place on a serving dish.
In a bowl, mix together 2-3 dessertspoons of light soy sauce (make sure you buy one that is naturally brewed), a couple of pinches of sugar and 1 dessertspoon of cooking rice wine. Pour this over the fish.
Scatter the fine strips of spring onion on to the fish: this is where the title of the dish comes from — bai he bai (white on white). If you would like to add more heat and colour to your midnight dish, cut the red chillis into very fine strips — like red silk ribbons — and also scatter on to the fish.
Heat the wok until it is hot and add 3 tablespoons of sunflower oil, heating the oil until it begins to smoke. You will see the smoke rising from the oil. Then pour the hot oil over the fish. There should be a very dramatic sound, like a clash of cymbals. The dish will only be successful if you hear this sound.
Serves 2

Allegra McEvedy — Claire's Brazilian Cheese Balls

Claire is one hard-working, hard-living chick. She got thrown in at the deep end as the manager of the big, bad, Bankside restaurant, of which she survived the hairy opening weeks on sparkly green eye-shadow alone. Claire cooked these for us at one of our First Tuesday monthly suppers when all of us Leon folk get together to eat, drink and be merry. They went down extremely well with a lot of cold beer, and made us all want to run naked along the beach, which isn't very surprising given their country of origin. However, if you're not in a position to run naked down the beach, we find they also make very good midnight feast food, especially if they're still a bit warm from the oven.

INGREDIENTS
• 175ml vegetable oil • 175ml water • 175ml milk • 1 tablespoon salt • 500g manioc starch (tapioca starch, must be from cassava; choose one labelled 'dulce', as this is the 'sweet' variety, rather than 'bitter' cassava — there is an enzyme that is produced in cassava that makes the cassava produce cyanide naturally and sweet cassava has less of this, although it has obviously been removed in production from both types) • 2 eggs • 275g cheese — 2 varieties (usually made with Alvao special selection cheese, made from cow's and goat's milk, and Casteloes original semi-soft cheese; ideally should be cheese locally made in Minas Gerais, but any hard cheese is OK)

METHOD
Pour the vegetable oil, water and milk into a large saucepan with some salt and bring to the boil, stirring from time to time. In a large mixing bowl place the manioc starch (or flour and cornflour combo). Add the hot liquid gradually to the starch and mix in with a spoon until all the liquid is used and a soft sticky mixture is formed (it should look a bit like mashed potato). Knead the eggs into the mixture, using your hands. It will be very sticky but not liquid; knead vigorously. Grate all the cheese as finely as possible and also mix in with your hands. Preheat the oven to 200°C/Gas 6. Oil your hands well and form the mixture into walnut-sized balls — they'll puff up a bit in the oven. Put the balls onto 2 well-oiled baking trays (remember their expansion plan) and place on the top and middle shelves of a hot oven. After about 20 minutes the top ones should be ready (golden brown), so take them out, then move the other tray up and give them another 5 minutes.
Makes about 30 balls

Daisy de Villeneuve's Plum Conserve

My favourite late-night food is taken from a Sesame Street cookbook I had when I was little and I continue to enjoy eating it. The recipe is yoghurt, crushed up digestives, honey and banana. I like to eat it in exotic locations, maybe on the beach with a boyfriend or a very good friend, listening to something '70s. When I was about 7 or 8 on the Brownie Pack Holiday we had a midnight feast and it was very exciting, even though I don't remember what we ate. But my chosen recipe dates back to a time when I was about 3 years old. I used to help my mother pick plums from the orchard next door to where we lived in Kent. She'd then make jam.

INGREDIENTS
• peeled rind of 2 oranges and 1 lemon, finely chopped • juice and pulp (without seeds) of 3 oranges and 1 lemon • 550g finely chopped raisins • 1.8kg sugar • 2.5kg plums, pitted and chopped • 4 peaches, pitted and chopped • 225g chopped walnuts

METHOD
Cook slowly on a low setting of your hob until thick, stirring frequently. Add chopped walnuts. Simmer another 10 minutes until 'set'. Pour into clean, warm glass jars with metal lids. Store in cool, dry place. Makes about 20 jars.
Served on warm toast with melted butter, straight out of the oven.
Perfect with a cup of tea.

KINVARA BALFOUR'S FAT LA BROWNIES

My younger sister and I had a midnight feast at home in London on a school night; we ate peanuts that we stole in handfuls from a cocktail party my parents were holding downstairs. Though we called it a midnight feast, I think it was probably around 9pm. I am sure if we had asked for them, Mum would have offered us bags of the things but theft seemed a far more exciting option at the time! A late-night feast now would probably be listening to Arcade Fire whilst dancing around the kitchen with my boyfriend Ricky.

I contemplate the idea of a midnight feast regularly as I love food. The brownies I have chosen are not that good for you but that's ok. You can't be healthy all the time, and you'd be very boring if you were.

INGREDIENTS
• 225g soft margarine • 110g plain chocolate (broken into small bite size chunks) • 170g plain flour • 1 teaspoon baking powder • 400g granulated sugar • 4 eggs • 1 teaspoon vanilla essence • 100g walnut halves • 100g white chocolate chips • 100g mini marshmallows

METHOD
Melt the chocolate in a bain-marie over a gentle heat and the margarine in a saucepan over a light heat. Mix the molten chocolate into the melted margarine. Take off heat and stir in the sugar. In a separate bowl, crack eggs and whisk until combined, add the vanilla essence. Pour mixture into molten chocolate and stir. Sift in the flour and baking powder, and fold gently into the mixture. Add white chocolate chips, walnut halves and marshmallows. Pour into a grease-lined baking tray and cook at 170°C for 40 minutes. Remove from oven and leave to cool. Cut into generous squares with a sharp knife. Serve warm with scoops of vanilla ice cream.
Serves 10

1

Fantastical Foods

HRH the Duchess of York, Sarah Ferguson's Baked Eggs, Coronation Chicken & Chocolate Cake

Midnight is a secret calm time which I have always liked; midnight and the small hours. I especially learned to appreciate it when my children were born and I would be up with them, feeding and settling them as every mother does. I loved holding a sleeping baby as I looked out over the comforting stillness of the night world around our home at Sunninghill Park: it was as if the night held us both safely in its arms. It goes without saying that because midnight is so magical, it always induces thoughts of a snack.

This chocolate cake is perfect for midnight snacking. I have tried probably every chocolate cake recipe there is, and still find this one to be the best. It is a moist and heavy cake that can also be served slightly warm with cream or ice-cream for a great dessert. I guarantee you will be asked for a copy of this recipe by anyone who tries it. It's a terrific favourite with my daughters Princess Beatrice and Princess Eugenie and indeed HRH Prince Andrew. When it was made for Princess Eugenie's 9th birthday party at Sunninghill, there was so much else to eat and to do that she was too excited to have more than a mouthful. So she crept down secretly at midnight into the kitchen and when I found it the next morning, she had taken every single chocolate button from the top of the cake.

On the other hand, if you want something that's little, quick, savoury and OK with your diet, there is nothing better than these baked eggs. The princesses and I adore them when we come in late. After an exciting, tiring evening all you want is something small to nibble.

The coronation chicken mixture is good to keep in the fridge as a standby for that late night moment. Just put some leftover cooked chicken in a bowl and fork over the mixture. Absolutely scrumptious at all times but especially after midnight.
(Written with the help of Princess Eugenie and Princess Beatrice)

Baked Eggs (Eggs en cocotte)
You will need: two ramekins (7.5cm) in diameter, well buttered, a roasting tin.

INGREDIENTS
• 2 eggs, large and fresh • 23g butter

METHOD
Preheat oven to 180°C/Gas 4. Fill and boil the kettle. Break an egg into each ramekin. Season well and top with a knob of butter. Place the dishes in the roasting tin and pour enough boiling water around the dishes to come half way up. Place the roasting tin in the oven and bake for 15 minutes. Alternatively, instead of adding butter, try adding a tablespoon of double cream or crème fraîche or perhaps some grated cheese.
Serves 2

Coronation Chicken

INGREDIENTS
• 2 onions • 50g butter • 8 dried apricots, soaked • large pinch of saffron strands finely grated rind of 2 lemons • 60ml thin honey • 75ml curry paste • 450ml dry white wine • mayonnaise • double cream or crème fraîche.

METHOD
Chop the onions then melt the butter and add the onions and sauté until softened. Add the apricots, saffron, lemon, honey, curry paste and wine. Simmer until the curry mixture is the consistency of thin chutney. Cool and blend in a food processor. Add mayonnaise and crème fraîche or double cream and mix to taste. Cook 4 chicken breasts in stock, drain and arrange on a plate then cover with mixture. Alternatively, use with cooked chicken.
Serves 2 or more

Chocolate Fudge Cake

You will need two 7 or 8-inch cake tins, buttered and base-lined with baking paper.

INGREDIENTS for the cake
• 100g plain chocolate • 100g demerara sugar • 300ml milk • 1 teaspoon bicarbonate of soda • 100g caster sugar • 100g butter, softened • 2 eggs, separated • 225g plain flour

INGREDIENTS for the icing
• 40g butter • 2 heaped tablespoons cocoa powder • icing sugar (the amount depends on how thick you would like your icing) • 2 tablespoons milk

METHOD

Preheat the oven to 170°C. Place the chocolate, milk and demerara sugar in a saucepan and heat gently, until the chocolate has melted and the mixture is very hot, but not quite boiling. Remove from the heat and stir in the bicarb. It will fizz up! Leave to cool slightly. Meanwhile, in a bowl, whisk the butter and caster sugar until light and fluffy. Beat in the egg yolks.

Add by degrees the warm chocolate mixture and the sieved plain flour, stirring well after each addition. In a clean bowl, whisk the egg whites to soft peaks and fold one spoonful into the mix to slacken it. Then gently fold in the rest. Pour the mix into the two tins and level the top. Bake for approx. 25 minutes until the surface of the cake springs back when pressed. Take out of the oven and cool for 10 minutes before sliding a palette knife around the edges and removing from the tins. Place on a cooling rack.

To make the icing, melt the butter in a medium saucepan and then sift in the cocoa powder. Cook, stirring for 1 minute, and then remove from the heat. Stir in the milk, and then an ounce at a time, stir in the sieved icing sugar. Continue adding the icing sugar until you have the consistency you desire and once the cake is cool, use to fill the cake and decorate the top. Arrange chocolate buttons on top of the cake. Heaven!

Serves 10 generously.

Filippo Tommaso Marinetti's Nocturnal Love Feast

In 1932, Filippo Tommaso Marinetti published *The Futurist Cookbook* advocating a new concept in food. An Italian artist, Marinetti believed that food should also be art and sought to combine meals with music, lighting and colour and such inedible objects as steel balls and aeroplane components. He denounced pasta as a pathetic Italian addiction to nostalgia and tradition, and believed that it made people lethargic and lazy. He argued that sustenance should come from pills, so that food could be free to become the raw material of art.

His Nocturnal Love Feast, detailed in *The Futurist Cookbook*, should ideally be eaten at midnight on the island of Capri. The feast starts with a large ham that contains a hundred different pork meats that have been soaked in milk for a week. Large oysters follow, each with eleven drops of Muscat wine from Syracuse mixed into its sea water. Then, a glass of Asti Spumante. A cocktail called the War-in-Bed should be the climax: an appetising blend of pineapple juice, egg, cocoa, caviar, red pepper, almond paste, nutmeg, and a whole clove, all mixed in yellow Strega liqueur. The feast itself is fantastical and engages the five senses. Although outrageously conceptual, Marinetti believed that it would easily seduce a woman. One such beauty responded, "I'm dazzled! Your genius frightens me!"

The owl and the pussycat went to the sea

Jane McMorland Hunter — Jared Ingersoll's Quince Royale

This recipe by Jared Ingersoll was inspired by Edward Lear's poem, *The Owl and the Pussycat*. The famous poem starts:
> "The Owl and the Pussycat went to sea,
>   In a beautiful pea-green boat,
> They took some honey, and plenty of money,
>   Wrapped up in a five pound note".

Once they reach the shores of their destination, the owl and pussycat are married. In celebration:
> "They dined on mince, and slices of quince,
>   Which they ate with a runcible spoon".

It's a romantic story about the marriage of two seemingly incompatible creatures and provides a delicious, fruity snack which produces leftover cordial as a bonus.

INGREDIENTS

• 1kg quinces • 2.4 litres of water • 170g caster sugar • 1 stick cinnamon
• 2 wide strips orange zest, this is easiest to do with a peeler • 2-4 whole
cloves, as you wish • 1 lemon
....

METHOD

Fill a bowl with water and add a squeeze of lemon. Peel the quinces, keeping
the skins. Cut the quinces into quarters or eighths, depending on their size
and remove their cores. Put the slices into the lemony water straight away
to prevent them from discolouring.

Fill a large, heavy-bottomed saucepan with 2.4 litres of water. Add the skins
and cores to the water, bring to the boil, then cover and simmer gently for
about 30 minutes. This is to extract the full flavour, and the pectin, which will
make the final liquid deliciously syrupy.

Strain the liquid, return to the saucepan and add the sugar, spices and orange.
Heat gently, stirring until the sugar has dissolved. Add the fruit, cover and simmer
for 2 hours. Check every so often to make sure the quinces are submerged,
adding more water if necessary. The fruit will gradually turn a lovely pink colour.
Remove the fruit and put into jars. It will be very soft and will break easily
so be gentle. Pour the syrup over, ensuring the fruit is covered, and refrigerate.
The left-over syrup can be made into a delicious cordial which you can serve
with water or, better still, sparkling wine. Add more sugar, depending how
sweet you want the syrup to be. I use half the amount in the original recipe.
Heat gently till the sugar has dissolved and then boil until the liquid has
reduced by about half. Leave to cool. Mix with fizzy wine, 1 part syrup to
3 parts wine.

Serves 6

Sophie Braimbridge's Baked Fish with Tomatoes & Spinach

The French call this technique of cooking in a parcel *en papillote* and traditionally greaseproof paper was used. But I find foil much easier to seal tightly, thus ensuring the steam released as the liquid in the foil heats up stays in the foil bag, creating a very succulent piece of fish. As the fish cooks, the foil expands, creating a parcel!

I often suggest this recipe for romantic meals as I have tied a ribbon into a bow like a wrapped present after cooking the fish in the foil. So, unless you are at a swingers party, you might want to halve the recipe!

This dish reminds me of my first courtship with my husband. He was sailing across the Atlantic and used to write to me about catching fish off the boat and how deliciously fresh it was. I used to so look forward to getting his letters (no email back then) and would pounce on the envelope, desperate to hear his news. He would write on the back of weather faxes that were beautiful pieces of art in their own right.

As someone who — by his own admission — is severely dyslexic, his writing was very hard to read. But luckily this never stopped him from writing down copious amounts of poetic thoughts and feelings, flowing down the pages, sometimes literally, as keeping a straight line was also hard to do!

Serving up a bright foil parcel wrapped with a red bow and opening it to release the delicious smell of the fish will always seem romantic to me.

Dear Sophie,

INGREDIENTS
• 800g trimmed fish such as monkfish or halibut, cut into 4 portions • 800g fresh spinach, washed, destemmed, cooked and squeezed dry • 2 heaped tablespoons of fresh marjoram or basil • 2 large flavoursome tomatoes, sliced, or cherry tomatoes halved • 2 tablespoons crème fraîche • 2 tablespoons of olive oil • salt and pepper

METHOD
Preheat the oven to 200°C/Gas 6.

Bone and skin your fish, or get the fishmonger to do it. But try to obtain 4 thick pieces of fish of the same size. If they vary in thickness, you will have to cook the thinner ones for less time, so maybe mark the papillottes so they don't get overcooked.

Tear 4 large pieces of foil and get your vegetables and other ingredients ready. Pour about half a tablespoon of olive oil onto the middle of each piece of foil and place a quarter of the squeezed spinach on top. Sprinkle with salt and pepper. Then place the monkfish on top of the spinach, scatter over some marjoram leaves, and put more salt and pepper onto the fish. Place about four slices of tomato on top of the fish and finally place about half a tablespoon of crème fraîche. Fold the foil over and seal the edges of the foil very well, so that no juices or air will escape in the cooking. It is often a good idea to use extra thick foil for this dish. Place the package onto a baking tray and put in the oven for about 15 minutes. If the foil is well sealed your package will balloon out once it is cooked. Serve immediately with unpeeled boiled new potatoes. It is often a nice idea to bring the foil to the table and allow your guests to open up their parcels themselves.

Serves 4

GERMAIN & LAURENT DEROBERT'S ONION SOUP

Running a cabaret means that we usually don't finish until dawn is breaking. After the long hours, we often feel the need for a little sustenance. A comforting dish, onion soup is ideal. It is also the perfect antidote to that one glass too many.

Legend has it that the soup was created by King Louis XV of France. Late one night, while staying at his hunting lodge, he discovered he had only onions, butter and champagne, so he mixed them together, thereby creating the famous French onion soup.

We have our own version of this recipe, which we concoct in our *dancing lodge*, after the last guests have left, cheekily putting to good use the odd half-drunk bottle of champagne to produce this convivial, hearty and fanciful soup.

INGREDIENTS
• 500g onions • 50g butter (or 3 tablespoons olive oil) • 1 tablespoon flour
• 1 or 2 or 3... glasses champagne • 1 litre stock • salt and pepper

METHOD
Peel and finely chop the onions. Heat the butter (or oil) in a large cooking-pot and brown the onions. Deglaze with the champagne then stir in the flour. Next add the stock and bring to the boil, simmering for half an hour. Add a pinch of salt (to taste) and lots of black pepper.

Optional: for a *gratinée* onion soup, place thin slices of brown toast on the top of the soup, cover with grated cheese (comté — or cheddar — for instance) and place under the grill for a couple of minutes before serving.

Serves 4

James Middleton's Red Velvet Cake Balls

My last memory of a midnight feast (not including raiding the fridge after a night out) was at boarding school. After the lights went out we sneaked into the pantry and found a box of Kit-Kats, made some hot chocolate, then bit off each end and sucked the hot chocolate up through the fingers, like a sort of biscuity straw. It was a messy but satisfying experience!

Working in the catering business means cooking at all hours. This one is perfect for a late night treat at parties.

INGREDIENTS
• 1 box of Red Velvet cake mix (or any cake mix you choose) • prepared cream cheese frosting (see recipe below) • 300g milk chocolate or bitter sweet chocolate (white chocolate works best) • packet of plastic lolly sticks or wooden BBQ skewers • selection of colour sugar sprinkles or icing tubes

METHOD
Bake the cake as directed on the box. After cake is cooked and cooled, crumble it into a large bowl. Mix the crumbled cake with the prepared frosting (it may be easier to use fingers to mix together but be warned it gets messy) until thoroughly mixed. Roll mixture into 1 inch sized balls and place onto parchment paper on a baking tray and allow to cool for several hours. You can speed this up by placing in the freezer. (Insert lolly sticks or cut the wooden skewers into lengths of 8cm and place in the middle of the balls — stick upwards). Melt chocolate in the microwave or in a metal bowl over a pan of simmering water, stirring occasionally until smooth. Remove the cakes from the fridge/freezer. One at a time, spoon the melted chocolate evenly over the cake ball. Place on wax or parchment paper to cool. While cooling, sprinkle over coloured sugar sprinkles. When set, use icing tubes to decorate. (Try experimenting with this recipe — use different cake mixes, put some food colouring in the melted white chocolate, wrap 4-5 on sticks in tissue paper to give a bouquet effect).

Cream Cheese Frosting
INGREDIENTS
• 125g cream cheese • 250g icing sugar • 90g unsalted butter • teaspoon vanilla essence

METHOD
Place all the ingredients in a mixing bowl and mix until smooth.

Banana & Rum

ZZZZ...

RAPHAËL COLEMAN'S BANANA FRITTERS FLAMBÉED IN RUM

Very simple recipe. 10 minutes max to make. Middle of the night. You wake up hungry. Desperately hungry. As you leave the bed your lazy partner asks blearily: "Wha... What are you doing?" As soon as they understand food is involved, they quickly say, "Oh well, while you're at it...". And you land yourself a full meal, tea and coffee, some biscuits and could you bring up my glasses (they're just in the living room)? If, out of self-respect or CBB (Can't Be Bothered) disease, you don't do all or even any of these things, here's something that will silence their protests as soon as they get a whiff of it.

INGREDIENTS

• 1 or 2 bananas per person, depending on how hungry you/they are • 35g of butter • good quality dark rum (not cocktail kind such as Malibu if you can help it) • cinnamon, nutmeg and/or ground cloves to taste

METHOD

Cut the bananas in half lengthways. Heat a large frying pan (preferably one that has more space than needed to accommodate your banana halves) for a few seconds before putting the butter in. Make sure the butter does not burn, or even go brown. Carefully put the bananas in so that the cut side is on the bottom of the pan. Allow them to cook for 3-5 minutes, until they are golden brown underneath. Flip the bananas over, carefully. At this stage they will be very soft, and if handled roughly, they will split, which doesn't change the taste, but makes them harder to handle and doesn't look very good on the plate. When they are almost done on the second side, you must work very fast to add all your extra spices. Be careful not to add too much, the taste is easily ruined. If the bananas are the same colour on both sides they are done and you must take them off the heat leaving the ring on. Take a ladle and pour in a small measure of your rum, then heat it gently over the flame. Do not leave the ladle too close to the flame, or it will catch fire on its own.

Here is the fun part. It is also very impressive if you pull it off right, especially if you have style and add a little flourish. Make anyone nearby stand back, pour the hot rum into the frying pan with the fritters, and while standing well back, set the liquid on fire. If you have added too much rum, the result will be burnt banana fritters, singed hair, blackened curtains, and if you're really stupid, a housefire. I can't stress this enough, GO EASY ON THE RUM. If you haven't royally messed up your wonderful dessert, then you must wait until the flames die down before serving the fritters. If you're a real pyromaniac, like me, or you don't want to get drunk at 3 in the morning, you can light the rum again and again until there is no alcohol left. Surprisingly, this doesn't spoil the taste of the rum, and you can fool anyone looking for a strong drink when you need them to stay sober. Voilà. Banana fritters flambéed in rum, one of my favourite recipes, and probably one of yours too now.

Serves 2

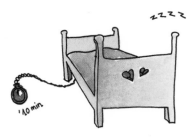

5

Food for Keeping You Awake

Welsh Rabbit Crumpets

Mark Hix's Welsh Rabbit Crumpets

My grandmother used to leave out a tin of Dorset knob biscuits and a big lump of blue vinney. I'd normally been out to the local club and the crumbs were everywhere the next day.

Nowadays, I normally crash out when I get home although we often invite friends spontaneously and get through several bottles of wine or partida tequila and snacks from the fridge (like my home smoked salmon or cured meats). I have a bad music collection so we normally end up with Santana. Another reason for eating late would be night fishing for sea trout with a headlamp — that normally gets a bit of an appetite going!

I'm not one for messing with the classics, but I do love toasted crumpets with this cheese topping. The other day I went to make some and found I was clean out of crumpets. A lesson to be learnt: always have some in the freezer. I've burrowed into the rabbit versus rarebit debate before, and I'm sticking to rabbit, the term used as far back as Hannah Glasse's day in the 18th century. She gives recipes for Scotch Rabbit, two for English Rabbit and one for Welch, yes Welch, rabbit. Whatever you call your poshed-up cheese on toast — or crumpets — it's delicious, and you can spice it up as much as you like.

INGREDIENTS
• 8 crumpets, toasted • 250g Caerphilly or Cheddar cheese, grated
• 2 egg yolks • 3 teaspoons Worcester sauce • 1 teaspoon English mustard
• 40ml double cream • salt and pepper

METHOD
Mix the cheese, egg yolks, Worcestershire sauce, mustard and double cream together and season. Toast the crumpets on both sides, spread the cheese mixture on top, about 1cm thick, and to the edges to avoid burning, and grill on a medium heat until nicely browned.
Serves 4

OLIVIA MORRIS'S VEGGIE SAUSAGE & HUMMUS SANDWICH

This feast is stolen from a midnight feast at a fellow fashion designer's house in London, circa 2003, and I am still feasting on it now. She was right — "It's the best sarnie you will ever taste".

INGREDIENTS
• 2 thick slices of bread (preferably brown and seedy) • a couple of grilled Tivali vegetarian 'hot-dog-style' sausages • a huge dollop of San Ambrosia hummus • 2 sweet plum tomatoes

METHOD
Toast the bread, grill the sausages, dollop the hummus onto the toast, split the sausages down the middle and load them on, pile on the tomatoes, squish it together and feast!
Serves 1

ANNIE MORRIS'S CHILLI SPAGHETTI

I have always loved spaghetti more than anything else. My mother made me a cake for my birthday when I was eight in the shape of a bowl of spaghetti and I was very disappointed that it was cake! I love coming home really late and making chilli spaghetti. Since I got engaged to Idris we have been making it a lot.

During the preparation I have a fight with myself about how wrong it is to eat at midnight, and spaghetti of all things! This continues just until I have finely chopped the chilli and garlic. Idris is my favourite person to have midnight spaghetti with. He always tells me it is the best one I have ever made!

INGREDIENTS
• 1 large red chilli • 1 clove of garlic • 4 tablespoons olive oil • 1 splash of white wine • more spaghetti than you think you need • generous sprinkling of Parmesan cheese

METHOD
Put the olive oil into a pan and heat. Add the chopped garlic and chilli. Meanwhile boil the spaghetti until al dente. Put a splash of white wine into the pan. Drain the spaghetti and mix with the chilli and garlic oil. Sprinkle with parmesan.
Serves 2

Tom Hodgkinson's Bacon Sandwich

From the age of about 17, my favourite place for a post-midnight snack was the Bagel Bakery on London's Brick Lane. My friend Rachel lived over that end of town long before it became fashionable, and it was she who introduced me to it. Always open and always convivial, the Bagel Bakery, a relic of the old Jewish East End, is a familiar feature on the London night owl's landscape: clubbers, mini-cab drivers and night shift workers mix there. It's one of those places where prim daytime etiquette evaporates, and, as is the case with night buses, everyone chatters away to each other. These good spirits are due of course to the varying states of intoxication that the punters are in, but also to that delicious after midnight feeling that we are in another world here, away from everyday worries, and we can be human, by which I mean neighbourly, friendly and cheerful.

The great 19th century reformer and agitator William Cobbett said that pretty much all human beings needed to be happy were what he called *the three B's*: beer, bread and bacon. I think he was spot on, and so my midnight feast would, without any doubt, be a bacon sandwich and a bottle of fine ale. The bacon would preferably be home-cured and come from our own pigs, maybe Saddlebacks. The rich butter would drip all over the place. The bread would be home-baked (using really good flour) and the beer would either be a nice dark brew like Barn Owl by the Somerset brewers, or Cotleigh, or the great Fuller's London Pride all the way from the Hogarth roundabout, in Chiswick.

INGREDIENTS
• home cured bacon, preferably saddlebacks (rich-tasting, good quality)
• lots of butter • home baked bread • bottle of beer

METHOD
Grill bacon. Apply butter generously to the bread. Place bacon between the bread. Wash down with beer. I imagine returning home after a long journey just after twelve, and finding this snack laid out for me on the kitchen table, with a lit candle next to it, like those magical meals in 'Beauty and the Beast'.
Serves 2

SOKARI DOUGLAS CAMP'S SUYA
(SLICES OF BEEF ON A SKEWER GRILLED ON A COAL FIRE)

A good midnight memory for me happened recently. I was in Nigeria for an art exhibition and symposium, the first in 17 years organised by the Nigerian government since FESTAC. After a long day of talking, dining and drinking, we went to a club at midnight. I saw scantily-clad performers who shook parts I had forgotten one could shake and Nigeria's answer to James Brown (72 years old) crept up to unsuspecting women on the dance floor as he sang and glued himself to them — like a leech doing energetic pelvic thrusts. It made the dancers laugh (oh! everybody laughed) and retreat quickly at the same time with embarrassment.

The night was scented and hot, the music was good and everyone seemed so at ease; even the Minister of Culture took to the dance floor, Travolta style, celebrating the achievement of pulling off this art fair, ARESUVA.

I have a CD of one of the popular songs of this visit, by one of the artists and I play it everywhere. It brings back the physical energy in that club, the triumph of the moment, all those dancers, dancing into the early hours, the excitement and joy, drinking Star beer and chewing Suya, a delicious combination which crowns any midnight moment in Nigeria.

INGREDIENTS
• thick slices of beef • ground peanuts • pepper

METHOD
Grill the slices of beef on a coal fire, or a griddle if cooked in a typical English kitchen. Dust the cooked beef with ground peanuts and pepper. Rather than cooked at home, however, the food is best bought in a take-away such as in the Walworth Road, south London or indeed from cafés and restaurants anywhere where there is a big Nigerian community.
Serves 1

6

Cooking by Moonlight

SAMANTHA CLARK'S CHORIZO
WITH SHERRY

My memories of eating late at night began with summer holidays in France when I was young. Nowadays any late-night moments are spent with my husband Samuel in our garden listening to Damien Rice. We had several midnight feasts at my school. My children also love the idea of a midnight feast but always sleep through till the morning.

INGREDIENTS
• 200g chorizo, suitable for cooking • olive oil • 75ml fino sherry

METHOD
Cut the chorizo in half lengthways and then into little bite-sized pieces. Place a frying pan over a medium heat and add a few drops of olive oil. You don't need very much as the chorizo will release its own oil. When the pan begins to smoke add the chorizo and fry, turning quickly when one side is coloured. This will take a matter of seconds. When both sides are crispy, add the sherry, watch out for the hissing, and leave for a few seconds to burn off the alcohol. Transfer to a dish and enjoy immediately. You can grill this chorizo just as easily, but omit the sherry.
Serves 2

Sir Arnold Wesker's Potato Pat

When I think about midnight feasts it's with a new girlfriend to the sound of Manuel de Falla's *Nights in a Garden of Spain*. Bach, though, reminds me most of midnight, because of midnight mass. My memory of eating midnight feasts takes me back to camp in the Wye Valley aged about 14. Everyone would have brought something with them from home, and come midnight, we'd share what we had, spreading everything out in the middle of the tent and picnicking on a blanket: hardboiled eggs, matzos, bridge rolls, cheese, salami, fruit cake and bars of chocolate.

This is not a slimming recipe but it's very tasty. I've eaten it once only, in a restaurant in Tokyo, so I've had to guess how it was done.

INGREDIENTS
• 2 medium sized potatoes • 1 medium sized onion • 2 cloves of garlic
• 225g of Mozzarella cheese • 50g butter • olive oil • optional ingredients
for serving with 'Pats': roast lamb, grilled steak or vegetables

METHOD
Dice the potatoes, halve then slice the onion and thinly slice the cloves of garlic. Boil the diced potatoes. While waiting for potatoes to become soft, lightly fry the onion and garlic in olive oil. Set aside. Strain the potatoes, and return them to saucepan. Gently fold the fried onion and garlic into potatoes in the saucepan. Don't make a mash of them, let the potatoes remain a little solid (though not, of course, raw). Separately fry the Mozzarella till soft and mixable. Fold into the mix of potato, onion and garlic. Season to taste.

Take it out of saucepan and, when cool enough, pat it into two circles, like thick pancakes. Melt butter till hot, short of burning. Fry and turn the two pats till each side is brown and crisp. Serve on its own or as a vegetable with roast lamb or grilled steak. You may need to fry the pats separately, in which case, you might need extra butter. Not difficult to gauge how much.
Serves 1

LADY CAROLE BAMFORD'S LEMONADE
FROM FRESH LEMONS

The last time I ate late was around Christmas when the moon was high in Barbados. We had lanterns in the trees, and the food and company were wonderful. Just writing about it now brings back many happy memories!

INGREDIENTS
• 4 unwaxed organic lemons • 100g sugar • water • thyme and mint to taste
• sugar to taste

METHOD
Take the 4 unwaxed organic lemons, wash the skins, and cut the lemons into chunks, cutting off the ends. Add to a food processor with 50g of sugar and water to cover them. Process to a mush, then strain, return the mush to the processor and add another 50g of sugar and a little more water. Whiz to a mush, and then combine with the first contents. Chill. When you wish to serve, top up with still or sparkling water, adding sugar if you need the mix a little sweeter. Delicious served with fresh thyme or fresh mint.
Serves 2

AC Grayling's Spicy Bean Burgers Covered in Thick Tomato Sauce

It is a custom among the Chinese to welcome, thank, or bid farewell to visitors by giving a banquet, invariably featuring favourite delicacies: Hundred-Year-Old Eggs; sea slugs; the webbed feet of ducks; fish-scented aubergine; Pocked-Marked-Face-Old-Woman tofu; twice-fried pork and much beside. This can sometimes be a trial for foreign visitors, and I'm sure that the Chinese are amused by the changes of colour and expression on their guests' faces when they are told what they have just swallowed (especially when from the foreigner's point of view it is something akin to dog's testicles or rat meat).

The banquet given for me by the Chinese Academy was, however, memorable for reasons additional to the exotic food. It was held in a room in the Zhong Nan Hai complex of the Forbidden City, on Jade Isle in the Central Southern Lake itself (which is what 'Zhong Nan Hai' means), on which giant lotus leaves and blossoms float, with ornamental trees along the walkways connecting the islands and the shore. The dinner served was one that the empress Ci Xi was wont to eat — a hundred different dishes, from some of which she took a small taste before sending them all back. This cuisine is known as Fangshan, meaning Imperial Cuisine, and is traditionally characterised by the best possible ingredients and the plainest names. This wouldn't have included the spicy bean burgers and thick tomato sauce that I recommend for a midnight feast.

Bean Burgers

INGREDIENTS

• 1 finely diced carrot • 2 tablespoons olive oil • 1 finely chopped clove garlic • 1 finely chopped half-clove sized knob of ginger • 1 small onion chopped very fine • 1 teaspoon each of mixed herbs, ground cumin, and ground coriander • Half a teaspoon each of paprika and chilli powder • 200g each of cooked red kidney beans and chick peas (in each case half of a 400g tin, rinsed and drained) • 1 level tablespoon of flour

METHOD

Mash the kidney beans and chick peas and leave ready. Boil the carrot until it just begins to soften. At the same time heat one tablespoon of the olive oil in a frying pan and add the garlic, ginger and onion until they are soft and lightly brown. Then add the spices, herbs and flour and stir continuously for one minute, ensuring that the flour does not burn. Mash this mixture into the waiting bean and chickpea mash, at the same time heating the remaining tablespoon of oil in the frying pan. Shape the mash into 4 burgers and fry them for 5-6 minutes each side or until done.

Tomato Sauce

INGREDIENTS

• tablespoon olive oil • 1 clove garlic diced • 1 clove-sized knob of ginger, chopped • 1 onion, chopped • 6 large ripe tomatoes • 1 tablespoon cornflour, approximately

METHOD

Nick the tomatoes with a sharp knife and blanch them in boiling water to remove the skins. At the same time, heat the oil in a pot and add the onion, garlic and ginger to soften and lightly brown. Chop or mash the blanched tomatoes and carefully place in the hot oil (it will sputter at first). Cook until the tomatoes are liquefied. Stir in cornflour to thicken. Season to taste; a little extra pepper is good.

Pour a covering of thick tomato sauce onto each bean burger and eat. They are healthy and tasty and fully vegetarian!

Serves 2

Matthew Line's Chargrilled Chicken

This is a really easy, low fat supper and was introduced to me by Penny Bingham, a great cook. It is simple, cheap and quick to concoct. And it tastes more exotic than it is! I made it up in Skye, when I was desperately trying to impress my wife to be. It was New Year's Eve and we had spent the evening with the locals first footing. They had entertained us with ballad after Scottish ballad and I had made a fool of myself by drunkenly trying to compete and sing a half remembered English folk song that stumbled to a close. In the early hours we returned to the tiny boathouse we were staying in — the sole building on a wide bay — and I cooked this meal to try and allay the effects of the alcohol. I remember the two of us eating wrapped in sheets by a wood-burning stove, listening to the rain belt down on the tin roof as we watched the glow of dawn grow pink on the sea.

INGREDIENTS
• 4 large chicken fillets • large tub of natural yoghurt • 2 teaspoons Garam Masala • 6 cloves garlic, crushed • 4 teaspoons finely grated fresh ginger • juice of 2 lemons • new potatoes • chopped fresh parsley • butter • green salad

METHOD
Score the chicken breasts and put into a bowl with the yoghurt, Garam Masala, ginger, salt pepper, lemon juice and garlic. Cover with cling film and marinate for 24 hours if possible. Place the fillets, topped with a dollop of the marinade, under a very hot grill and cook fast, turning the fillets once. Depending on the thickness of the fillet, 4 minutes a side will probably do it. You want a juicy moist chicken inside and speckles of slightly charred chicken on the surface. Serve with buttered new potatoes and chopped parsley and a simple green salad.
Serves 4

Yasmin Mills' Chilled Raspberry Whip

At 8 years old I was occasionally allowed to stay up late, as a treat, to watch TV with my parents while eating a particularly delicious chicken and rice dish that my mother used to make.

Now, midnight feasts for me are having crunchy nut cornflakes and ice cold milk with my daughters as a treat before bed.

This recipe is my little girl Maddie's invention. It is a simple chilled fruity pudding that doesn't require any cooking. It is a particularly refreshing, scrumptious treat to serve after dinner in the summer or to make when you get in after a night out.

INGREDIENTS
• 200g chilled raspberries • 100g chilled strawberries • 500ml chilled double cream • 1 tablespoon of icing sugar • you can substitute the strawberries with blueberries if you like. However, I think the classic British summer strawberry and raspberry combination, which was chosen by my little Maddie, works best in this pudding.

METHOD
Remove any stalks and leaves from the strawberries, then quarter them and put to one side. Pour the cream into a bowl and whisk, with a hand or electric whisk, until the cream becomes stiff. Add the icing sugar and raspberries to the cream and whisk for a minute or two more. Then, gently stir in the quartered strawberries before distributing equally between 2 bowls or glasses. As you should use ingredients that come straight out of the fridge, there is no need to chill this pudding and you can enjoy eating it immediately!
Serves 2

7

Inspired Feasts from Childhood

Split
Mealy
Pudding

Scrambled eggs &French
Nights

Rose Prince's Split Mealy Pudding, Scrambled Eggs & Cress

English children so often go to bed before daylight ends in summer. My brothers, sisters and I would lie in bed while the adults ate separately from us, and we could hear the tinkle of glasses, wine being poured, and the clink of knives and forks as we fell asleep. But when we visited my grandmother who lived in France, it was different. We became French children and sat up with her and her friends. We ate what they ate and drank water with a drop of wine in it. It was so grown up — and civilised. After pudding, the watery wine would perform the intended trick, and we'd sleepily slope off to bed, just around midnight. I think those holidays in France taught me how to live, and also that children are a part of the family that should be seen and heard. It did no harm to our palates, either, giving an early food education that has stayed with all of us and which we are now trying to pass on to our own children.

After dinner we'd sometimes go indoors to escape the mosquitoes and my grandmother would unlock her chocolate cupboard. She was addicted to Suchard Milko and terrified we'd steal it and she would run out, hence the security. She hated nostalgia and always bought albums (vinyl) of her favourite bands. It was the '70s and the Rolling Stones and David Bowie were her favourites. We sat up for what seemed like hours, nibbling chocolate, listening to music and cracking very silly 'in' jokes, teasing each other. My grandmother drank Four Roses Bourbon on the rocks. She died in 1993, and I wish I could bring her back, and those nights.

I am not really aware of midnight as a deadline for anything because I love to sit up late. I rarely eat after twelve, though, or go in for midnight feasts as such, but will sometimes pick at leftovers while doing the washing up. If I do plan a midnight feast it is breakfast: scrambled eggs, grilled bacon and kidneys, toast and marmalade. Try it after a long night of partying and you will feel all the better for it next day.

Mealy pudding consists of a natural sausage skin, about 30cm/12 inches long, filled with oatmeal and meat juices. Sliced and fried, it is ready to be put on a plate with some creamy scrambled eggs. The cress greens it all up a little, but just to serve. Serve with brown toast.

....

INGREDIENTS
• 1 tablespoon olive oil • 4 mealy puddings, sliced into 2cm chunks • 9 eggs, lightly beaten • 55g unsalted butter • 2 tablespoons double cream • 2 punnets of mustard and cress • sea salt

....

METHOD
Heat the oil in a large frying pan and fry the mealy puddings over a gentle heat until golden on both sides. While they cook, scramble the eggs. Season the beaten eggs with salt, then melt the butter in a saucepan. Pour in the eggs and cook over a low heat, stirring with a wooden spoon until the egg begins to thicken on the base of the pan. Scrape at the base with the spoon and continue to cook until the egg is thick and creamy. Do not allow it to get too solid — before this happens, remove from the heat, add the cream and stir. The mealy pudding should be ready by now. Serve it on warmed plates with a pool of scrambled egg and the toast, mustard and cress on the side.
Serves 4

Tara Palmer–Tompkinson's Chocolate Cornflake Cakes

When I was in boarding school, we had our kitchen, which we mainly used to prepare midnight feasts. They helped me revise for my A–Levels!

INGREDIENTS
• 50g butter • 50g golden syrup • 50g Suchard Express chocolate powder (any powder will do but this is my preference — available at Harvey Nichols on the 5th floor) • box of cornflakes

METHOD
Heat all the ingredients in a saucepan. Once all heated and melted mix with cornflakes and put into little cake cases. Then put in fridge to set.

Sian Lloyd — Lavinia Vaughn's
Rice Pudding

My childhood home in Neath, South Wales, was dominated by the vagaries of a coal-fired AGA. When it ran hot, there'd be a scramble to make scones, when it was slow, my father would turn his hand to meringues and rice pudding. He did most of the cooking at home and was a very creative and generous chef.

This meant there was always a glut of goodies on offer and no meal was ever complete without a choice of at least two or three desserts. To this day, I blame that giant deep green AGA for my serious sweet tooth!

As the eldest of three children, I would often regale my sister Ceri and my brother David with stories I made up. They would sneak into my bedroom and I'd act out weird and wonderful scenarios for hours on end, well into the early hours of the morning. Afterwards, I'd lead the raid on the fridge and sneak back upstairs with a tray of goodies for our late night feast. Our favourite was always rice pudding, thick and creamy with a huge dollop of my father's home-made strawberry jam in the middle. And it remains one of my favourite puds to this day, taking me back to those delicious times.

INGREDIENTS
• 100g pudding rice • 25g unsalted butter • 50-75g caster sugar • 1 strip orange zest • 1 vanilla pod • 1 litre semi skimmed milk • 2-3 tablespoons double cream

METHOD
Rinse the rice in cold running water.
Melt the butter in a solid based saucepan, add the rice and stir to coat in the butter. Add 50g sugar, the orange zest and the vanilla pod. Add one third of the milk and bring to the boil, stirring occasionally. Reduce the heat and simmer until nearly all of the milk has been absorbed. Add the milk a little at a time, stirring occasionally until the rice is tender. Discard the orange zest and vanilla pod (scraping out the seeds first) and add more sugar if needed.
Stir in the double cream.
Served 2

JOANNA WEINBERG — CHARLIE'S SHORTBREAD

Midnight feasts for me will always be associated with childhood Christmases in South Africa with my grandmother. She had one of those giant walk-in fridge rooms with a great metal door. Inside were all manner of feasts — fruit like you'd never believe growing up in England in the '70s: sunset red nectarines and fragrant honeydew melons; watermelons so giant they were difficult even for a grown up to carry alone. There were ripe, buttery avocados to eat straight from the skin with salad dressing pooled into the hole left by the stone.

There was a never ending supply of cold roast chicken to pull straight off the carcass and eat with greasy fingers. The kitchen smelt of baking. Her cook, Charlie, made the most crumbly shortbread imaginable, it literally used to disappear on the tongue. The only thing my grandmother has cooked in her whole life (South African whites of her generation simply never went into the kitchen) was with me — coconut ice. We would upend a packet of desiccated coconut into a pan of condensed milk and add a huge amount of sugar and a few drops of cochineal. But best of all were the mini chicken pies we would pick up fresh from the farm shop, so juicy and buttery that grease would run down your chin. Granny would gather up a selection of all these wonderful things, reset the clock, and wake us up at about 9 o'clock to feast on reheated chicken pies, multicoloured melon balls, avocado halves and coconut ice, and that would still be my ideal feast now. This recipe is easy to remember as the volumes go 1–2–3. You can roll it out thicker for a stodgier biscuit, but you'll need to cook for a few minutes longer.

INGREDIENTS
• 100g caster sugar • 200g butter • 300g flour • pinch of salt

METHOD
Cream the sugar and the butter. Sieve the flour and the salt, and mix together with the butter to make a soft dough, being careful not to overwork it. Wrap in Clingfilm and allow to rest in the fridge for 1 hour, and then half an hour at room temperature, before your roll it out.
Preheat the oven to 160°C. Roll the dough out to 1/2 cm thickness and cut into whatever shapes you like — cookies, crescents, or just fingers (I find this can be very difficult as the dough is so short it breaks up, so I often end up with the strange, rough-edged shapes that it naturally breaks up into, and I've decided to like them). Line a baking sheet with parchment and place the biscuits on the parchment.
Bake for 15-20 minutes until golden. Remove from the oven and after 5 minutes, carefully lift on to a rack. They will still be a bit soft but will turn crispy as they cool.
Serves 6

CHLOE LONSDALE'S CRISPY CRACKLES

I have very fond memories of hosting Teddy Bears Tea Parties for all my friends when I was 6 or 7. We would sit around the break-fast bar of the kitchen in my childhood home and eat the Crispy Crackles that I would have made with my Mum earlier that day.

INGREDIENTS
• 100g unsalted butter • 1/3 cup golden syrup • 2/3 cup drinking chocolate
• 3 cups cornflakes • handful of mini marshmallows

METHOD
In a bain-marie melt the butter and chocolate and then add the golden syrup and marshmallows. Take off the heat and pour on to the cornflakes; mix and stir in. Then put a tablespoon of the mixture in each of the paper fairy cake cases. Let them cool and put in the fridge.
Serves 6

Dawn Porter's Rye Bread & Goat's Cheese

When we were kids, my sister, Jane and our cousins James and Charlotte used to have midnight feasts all the time. We would lay all of our duvets and pillows out on the floor and scoff sweets and Marmite sandwiches until we felt sick. For some reason, I was always the last one to go to sleep. Probably because I was the only one still eating! When everyone else was sleeping, I used to get as close to my cousin as I could. She was a year younger than me and I loved her more than anything. I had this thing in my head about how when animals are born, they think the first person they see is their mummy. So I used to position my face right up against hers and fall asleep thinking that when she woke up in the morning, my face would be the first thing she saw, and she would love me more than anything else. It never worked out that way though. I don't mean the love bit, we are best friends to this day, I mean the face bit... I usually woke up with her bum on my nose instead! These days, I always have a snack before I go to bed. When I was growing up we had beehives in our garden, and my parents made honey. I love it, and it always comforts me and makes me feel relaxed. So, now this is my favourite midnight feast snack. Rye bread and goat's cheese with honey.

INGREDIENTS
• two slices of rye bread • salty butter • goat's cheese • runny honey

METHOD
Take the rye bread, butter it thickly then squash the goat's cheese all over it. On top of that I dribble a tablespoon of runny honey. I wash it all down with a cup of Red Bush tea, and sleep like a baby. Perfect!
Serves 1

With special thanks to
Kate Hadley from Springboard
& Laetitia Rutherford from Mulcahy Conway Associates,
as well as
Michael Day my very patient friend,
Books for Cooks and Sally Hughes for her encouragement.

My Own Midnight Feast

© Published by Les éditions du Delirium
23, rue de la République – 84000 Avignon – France
www.ledelirium.net
contact@ledelirium.net

Layout: Julien Gaillardot

Printed in France in January 2010 by Delta Color

ISBN: 978-2-9529370-6-1

Dépôt légal : février 2010

9 782952 937061